A Bridge of Light

How to Pray to Angels

By

Melissa R Sklar

Published in America by Harp Lady Books

Ann Arbor, Michigan

USA

Email: harpladybooks@gmail.com

Website: www.abridgeoflight.com

A BRIDGE OF LIGHT: How to Pray to Angels

Copyright©2023 by Melissa R. Sklar

ISBN (Book): 9798864007556

Cover Art: Oh-So-Hapi,© Mara Friedman, newmoonvisions.com.

Graphic Design: Christine Kos, www.christinekos.com.

TABLE OF CONTENTS

FOREWORD

Why worry when you can pray and if you are going to worry it makes no sense you pray. This sums up the importance of prayer in our lives. I believe that each of us is responsible for the well-being of our soul and that correct knowledge helps us to do just that. I have been a psychic medium, shaman, spiritual/traditional healer, and counselor for more than thirty-three years and have written several books on reincarnation and the expiation, advancement and restoration of the soul as instructed and inspired by my Guides. In one of these books, I briefly cover the topic of prayer which is very important in expiating, advancing and restoring our soul. I know the power and necessity of prayer. And so when my dear friend and fellow Rescue Soul, Melissa, during one of our conversations mentioned that she had channeled much information on prayer, with the title as given by the Angels, *A Bridge of Light: How to Pray to the Angels,* a light bulb lit up in my head. My heart skipped a few beats as I heard the words "beautiful book" whispered in my ears by my guides. I knew that the information would be accurate and its veracity unquestionable because it was channeled through the mediumship of Melissa, a psychic reader, medium, channeler and past life reader extraordinaire. I knew that many in the world could use this information to make their lives better. I had the great privilege of having a front-row seat watching Melissa diligently transform channeled information into a "beautiful book." The Higher Powers wanted mankind to have this information on prayer and chose Melissa, the Rescue Soul that she is, to deliver their message of how to use prayer to access the bridge of light to a Higher Self and Divine consciousness. They knew that she would deliver it exactly as it was given without allowing ego to deviate from or alter it.

Indeed, prayer is personal and Melissa emphasizes this by providing us with a brief outline of prayer and its resonance to each zodiac sign. She also allots space at the end of the book to create our own personal prayer or to transcribe one that resonates with us. As a matter of fact, we could create more than one prayer, each for a different purpose.

*After reading this beautiful book **A Bridge of Light: How to Pray to the Angels**, channeled by Melissa Sklar, you will have no need to worry because you will gain a full understanding of prayer. You will develop a very good relationship with the Angels, know why some prayers are not answered and how to augment prayer to make it more meaningful. You will gain more agency over your life. You will worry less. You will find more peace in what is at times a "too-busy" world. Prayer will provide you with one of the tools with which to care for the well-being of your soul. Indeed, why worry when you can pray.*

- **Winnifred Davis**

Psychic Medium/Shaman and Author

Why must people kneel down to pray? If I really wanted to pray I'll tell you what I'd do. I'd go out into a great big field all alone or in the deep, deep woods and I'd look up into the sky—up—up—up—into that lovely blue sky that looks as if there was no end to its blueness. And then I'd just feel a prayer.

— L.M. Montgomery, 1908

Help is a prayer that is always answered. It doesn't matter how you pray—with your head bowed in silence, or crying out in grief, or dancing. Churches are good for prayer, but so are garages and cars and mountains and showers and dance floors. Years ago I wrote an essay that began,...Some people think that God is in the details, but I have come to believe that God is in the bathroom.

—Anne Lamott, 2004

We tend to use prayer as a last resort, but God wants it to be our first line of defense. We pray when there's nothing else we can do, but God wants us to pray before we do anything at all.

Most of us would prefer, however, to spend our time doing something that will get immediate results. We don't want to wait for God to resolve matters in His good time because His idea of 'good time' is seldom in sync with ours.

— Oswald Chambers, 1935

INTRODUCTION

Prayer is a conversation with the Divine.

Prayer is a connection to the Divine.

Prayer is a request of the Divine

Prayer is surrender to the Divine

Prayer is communion with the Divine

Prayer is reverence for the Divine

Prayer is recognition of the Divine

Prayer is remembering the Divine

Prayer is loving the Divine and being loved by the Divine.

Prayer is what links us

Prayer is what blesses us

Prayer is what finds us in the dark

Prayer is what opens a door.

Prayer is how we rise up

Prayer is how we transcend.

I to Thee and Thee to me.

My heart to your Heart

My will to Thy Will

Your Ear to mine.

My soul to Thine.

To the Angels of the Sun

And the Angels of the Moon

And the Angels of Stars

And the Angels of Earth

And to the Angels of the Day

And the Angels of the Night

The Angels who have always been

And the Angels that will always be

Prayer is always a bridge of light.

It is how we find each other.

I was not really brought up to believe in a personal God per say. I was raised in a Jewish household and God seemed very unknowable out there not involved in the mundane affairs of humans. My Judaism was more of a cultural touchstone, our prayers and practices unifying us in a common whole with a shared inherited heritage. It was all very abstract to me and being a philosopher and a seeker of truth from a young age I became an atheist at the age of fourteen because nothing at that time made any sense to me spiritually. So when I began experiencing and acknowledging the existence of angels as real entities in my life it was quite a surprise! I am forever an empiricist. I must experience something to believe in it.

That being the case, I have always had a sense of being connected to Nature and that Nature was a sentient force. I cannot say how I knew; the way a child just knows I guess. I felt the energy that was outside myself but also within me, flowing through me. I took it for granted and did not connect it to what people called Divine until I was much older. As a young adult, a friend introduced me to the music of Lisa Thiel and the worship of the Goddess who is intimately connected to Nature. That was the aha click of what the Divine meant for me. It had been forming for some time germinating in my mind but the epiphany came then.

However, the real communication for me happened almost simultaneously when a book called *To Hear the Angels Sing* by Dorothy McLean (1980) almost literally fell into my hands when I was wandering around a used book shop and a fellow Flower Essence practitioner taught me how to use a pendulum which became a very useful tool for muscle testing the remedies myself and my clients needed. McLean (1980) brought into my consciousness the communication with the Devic Spirits of Nature and the Angels that work with the Divine Realm of Nature. It would turn out the use of the pendulum would open up the channels to direct communication with the Spiritual World.

I recall at that time that there was a confluence of experiences that brought into my consciousness the concept of Guardian Angels guiding us through our lives though I cannot pinpoint all of them. One of the most significant events was a dream I had in which I was sitting on a bench by a river and beside me was a beautiful ethereal looking woman. She was bringing my attention to sacredness of the green river water. Shortly after that dream, I decided to ask my pendulum if she was one of my Guardian Angels. The answer was "Yes she is!" That was how my first introduction to my Guardian Angels began.

I was blessed to meet my Guardian Angels that day and over time my other Spirit helpers. It was an organic experience. It just happened without preconceptions. I cannot explain it any other way. I had no expectations or ideas about who the Angels were. I just suspended belief and put myself into a state of openness and curiosity. I had a million questions and using the pendulum as an aid to receive the answers, I asked as many and whatever questions I wanted.

I taught myself to listen in different ways, sometimes intuiting, sometimes hearing, sometimes seeing, and sometimes feeling what was being told to me, especially in my chakras. The better I was able to be open to receiving the answers and the more I worked on myself to become a clearer channel, the more accurate the information I received.

My Guardians encouraged me to ask as many questions as I desired and I realized that they were hungry for communication, involvement and interaction with us, that indeed that was their vocation and desire. And so it is for all of us with all of our Guardian Angels. In that way over time I became aware that the Archangels also wanted to work with us this way and at this time of our spiritual awakening and evolution we are to be working with them more intimately and personally than ever before, especially through prayer.

That is how this book came into genesis, as an answer to the question that has been circling around in my mind for a very long time: How to pray to the Angels? Inspired by this thought, I asked my Spirit Guides directly how they would instruct me and others to pray to them in the most effective manner. The following chapters are a result over time of the answers I received.

The first chapter addresses the question "What is prayer?" The second chapter addresses the question "What are Angels?" The third chapter addresses the seven Archangels who guard the seven chakras and the part they specifically play in prayer. In these chapters each individual Archangel allowed me to channel them to the best of my ability regarding their role related to their chakra of angelic resonance and responsibility.

The fourth chapter speaks to Divine Timing as it relates to prayer. Divine Timing is so often a conundrum to us mortal humans so it was very helpful for me to hear and transcribe their thoughts on the matter.

The fifth chapter outlines and emphasizes the importance of the role prayer has played throughout time and into the present.

Finally, in the sixth chapter, the angels offer three significant ways to augment prayer in your daily life.

I have also included a brief outline of prayer and its resonance to each Zodiac sign and well as a prayer journal where you can record your own experiences and thoughts on prayer. You can also use it as a space to transcribe your own prayers and the prayers you have learned that resonate with you. Remember there are no rules, expectations or restrictions. Be inspired! But also a reminder that the most effective prayer and the prayer best heard by the angels is a prayer that comes from the heart.

CHAPTER ONE
PRAYER

Prayer opens the spirit to Divine Love through surrender of the Individual Consciousness to Universal Consciousness. Prayer creates an energetic stream of communication between the supplicant, the Angels and the Divine. It is a powerful vibratory spiritual awakener. Prayer allows for a seismic shift in our energetic field changing its resonance in a way where it becomes more easily accessible to the Angelic and Divine Realms.

What is prayer but an arrow of concentrated light shot through the dark of our longing to the heavens above? As the arc of the arrow flies through time and space it creates a spiritual bridge on which your innermost thoughts and desirescan traverse through the dimensions to the realm of Divine Spirit. It opens the way through for individual communion with the Cosmos.

The practice of open-hearted prayer allows humans to be more conscious of this process so that humans can better understand the true nature of prayer. The practice of prayer itself helps individual hearts open to the Divine Heart and encourages you to make your requests and desires known to Divine Source without attachment or expectation. When you pray in this way, it is easier for the Angels to hear and fulfill your requests.

It is the Angels that are the prayer catchers, the mediums between Divine Consciousness and human consciousness. It is important to note that not all prayers can be answered in a timely manner if at all. There are so many factors at play but the most important is a Divine Ordinance that the manifestation of prayer is in accordance with the highest good of all. On a human scale of time and evolutionary purpose certain outcomes must play out. There is always a higher synergy that can be hard as a human to fathom sometimes in this interplay of what we called fate.

Forms of magic and invocation that try to circumvent Higher Divine order can be extremely dangerous and harmful not just to the individual involved but to the higher order and balance of collective evolution. It is only when we can see things from a Cosmic Perspective such as when we are in-between transitions of our incarnations that we can ultimately understand the reasons and ramifications of our fate.

Prayer is not a coin in a Cosmic Vending Machine. With only desire, expectation and hunger for the thing requested, the real purpose of prayer cannot be fulfilled because prayer in essence is an offering of love and surrender to a higher power/consciousness without expectation and in full humility and release.

Prayer involves not just our relationship with the Angelic Realms and Divine Realms but our relationship with our Higher Self, the over-soul of all our incarnations. It asks us to rise to a more transcendent consciousness so that even if the answer to the prayer is not an outward manifestation, it can still allow for a deeper and more complete awareness and understanding of the inner and outer workings of the Universe and our place in it. In doing so, even without outward manifestation, it has fulfilled its own purpose in just that transcendental leap in growth and connection with our Higher Self and the Angels.

In other words, although one of the functions of prayer has always been perceived, and rightly so, as a vehicle that opens the way for our needs and desires to be met, ultimately most important function of prayer is to enhance our relationship with the Divine Source. It is one of the most crucial ways by which we communicate with the Divine Realms. Prayer is our connection to Divine Consciousness. It is a channel through which Divine Light and Love can manifest on Earth.

Prayer helps build a bridge of light through which access is given to Divine Will and allows the flow of Divine Consciousness to merge with the Earthly and Soul realms. In this way, the frequent practice of prayer in our daily life can make it so our life itself becomes a prayer, transforming us into a vehicle for the manifestation of the forces of Divine Love, Divine Light and Divine Will on Earth.

There really is no prescribed way to pray. Everyone prays in their own way. We pray in churches, synagogues, mosques, temples, courtyards, woods, by rivers, in our houses, on mountains, in circles, in congregations, with our families, with friends, with nature, in groups or alone. Some of us meditate in prayer; some of us sing, some of us drum or pray in silence. Some light a candle, some pray by the moon or the light of the sun, rising or setting, in a grove of trees or in our beds before we rise or sleep.

Some of us use ancient prayers left to us by our ancestors, in written word in our various sacred texts or known to us by word of mouth or passed down through lullabies. Some of us make up our own prayers. All prayers are powerful and are heard by our Angels, said out loud or in thought but the most powerful and resonant are those that come from our hearts, said in humility and without expectation or condition, in gratitude and without attachment.

We must ask ourselves to understand and accept even at our most worried and desperate need, that prayer works in mysterious ways and acquiesce to Divine Timing, without entitlement or anger, without malice of forethought and bitterness.

We seek to understand the karmic nature of our predicaments and accept accountability for our circumstances but at the same time allow ourselves the suspension of belief and cynicism. In this way, we give permission so that Angelic intervention can and so often miraculously does allow for the answers to our prayers for the highest good of ourselves and for all.

***Note on Prayer: My favorite way to pray: Light a candle and then either standing or sitting find my center, raise up my hands to the sky and then put my hands together with the tips of my fingers at my brow chakra with my head bowed.

I then ask the Angels and the Divine Spirit for the things that I need help with both for myself, others, the planet and all sentient beings. Then I give thanks for all the blessings granted to me.

Finally, I like to end my prayers by saying "May this or something far better now manifest for the highest good of all concerned. Amen."

What is your preferred method? Find what works and resonates best for you.

CHAPTER TWO
WHAT ARE ANGELS

Angels are emanations from the most high. They were here before the Earth was born, before time and before duality. They are creations from the very heart of the Divine Matrix which is the energetic Mother of all life. They are made of love and of light as we all are but they resonate with the highest frequencies of all that is. Their minds, will and hearts are aligned with the highest good of the Meta verse and all that dwell within.

Their purpose is to be of service and to assist all sentient beings to become aligned with and fulfill their highest purpose. They are the bridges of light between us and Divine Consciousness. They are here to assist us in aligning ourselves and manifesting Divine will, love, light and life on Earth.

Angels are always with us throughout our earthly incarnations. They do hear our prayers and they do know our hearts but because of the fundamental birthright humans have been given of *free will*, they are limited on how much they can intervene for our own good especially as adults. Angels need to be invoked, to be asked, and that invocation is the act and communication of what we know as prayer. If we ask for their intervention and if and only if it is for the highest good, then they can truly manifest miracles in our lives.

The act of prayer, however we choose to pray, is the initiation of our intentional relationship with them. It starts the conversation and lifts us up to their vibration so the Angels can merge with our magnetic field to bring the fruition of the manifestation into being.

According to my guides, there are all kinds of angels who act as helpers. They will help you with almost anything you can think of. There are healing angels, abundance angels, angels who actually can help you when you are house hunting and angels who can help you with common house hold needs like electrical problems, plumbing, water leaks, garden angels, car angels and so on and so on. I have tried this out in prayer and it has worked amazingly well.

For instance, if I am having technological problems with my computer, I will pray to the angels of technology for assistance and often miraculously, what seemed like an impossible series of glitches clear up and things start working again.

I highly encourage people to reach out to the angels at hand. That is what they are here for which is simply to be of assistance to humans and always for our highest good and the highest good of all.

What are Guardian Angels

I love to introduce people to their Guardian Angels and I bless the day I was introduced to mine. They are truly our closest spiritual family. The Guardian Angels usually have been with us many lifetimes and will be with us many more. They resonate perfectly with our unique spiritual and vocational purpose. Unlike the majority of other angels, our Guardian Angels only belong to us and us to them.

The Guardian Angels tell me that we meet in between life times and we are drawn to each other because we perfectly resonate with each other. Yes, we as a collective humanity are all one but each of us has their own unique part to play in the symphony that is the human race and purpose. Our Guardian Angels are our very own personal shepherds and gardeners that are with us to accompany us on our very special evolutionary journey on the trail of incarnation lifetime after lifetime. No two souls' journeys are the same.

Another very unique attribute our Guardian angels possess is usually one lifetime incarnated as a human on earth although not with the humans they serve. The Angels are not on an evolutionary journey like we are which is why that incarnation does not involve karma. Instead, its purpose is so that they can understand the human psyche better and acquire spiritual gifts useful for the life path of their charge.

The Guardian Angels say that angelic and human consciousnesses are very different. Human nature as we know is complex, dualistic and often unpredictable and paradoxical with free choice whether to bend to our higher or lower vibration at every juncture. We are always in flux, On the one hand, we are pulled forward by self-actualization and self-discovery and a yearning to be one with our Higher Self and the Divine. On the other hand, we can also be pulled backwards by fear, anger, jealousy, ego and a desire to conform.

Angels fly above the fray as they are from the same source and resonance as the Divine and their vocation is truly to serve us. To be able to spiritually walk and work so closely with us with compassion, empathy and understanding from their own experience on Earth makes our Guardian Angel's human

11

incarnation invaluable. Furthermore, they appear to us as their human persona manifested from their earthly incarnation including their name, appearance as well the gifts, talents and skills that they acquired during that life time which is a wonderful blessing to us.

I highly encourage you to work as closely as you can with the your Guardian Angels and I want to assure you that your Guardian Angels are very eager to be of service and love to be acknowledged. They are amazingly accessible and encourage you to address your prayers to them as well as the other Angels because they can answer your prayers as well.

WHAT ARE ARCHANGELS

The Archangels are the 'Holiest of the Holies', the highest of the high amongst all Angels. They possess a multiplicity of 'super powers'. For instance, they can work with everyone individually at the same time. The Archangels are guardians of the Meta verse (the Universe that contains all universes) and holders of the sacred keys to portals between the dimensions. They are overseers of the space-time continuum and directly manifest Divine Will on Earth. Their wings span the galaxies and their love and compassion embrace all of us into infinity. Each Archangel has a special affinity and purpose related to our chakras which are also portals are connecting us to the Earth and to the Divine.

CHAPTER THREE

ARCHANGELS

The Seven Archangels most intimately involved with the seven main chakras of the human energy field have graciously given the author channeled detailed information for us regarding their roles and gifts on this matter. These are the *Archangels Ezekiel, Ariel, Gabriel, Raphael, Michael, Uriel and Chamuel.*

ARCHANGEL EZEKIEL

Archangel Ezekiel is the guardian of the First Chakra. He also has a special affinity with the Fourth and the Seventh Chakras. He emanates red light. He would also manifest with purple and or gold light but red light is his overriding color of origin.

Ezekiel comes through with the main element of fire. His staff is made of flame. His sword is made of fire and he wears a red cape pinned with a fleur de lis brooch made out of rubies and diamonds.

Ezekiel rules the first chakra with solar influence in conjunction with Mars (as if the Sun and Mars are conjunct). He mediates the cardinal flow of primal energies and sexual impulse.

Archangel Ezekiel is also the guardian of the Kundalini which is the seat of the spiritual energy or life force located at the base of the spine. It is often symbolized by the metaphor of a cobra energetically rising through all the chakras and when fully engaged, causes the crown chakra to open like a lotus to the light of the Divine Sun.

Archangel Ezekiel is the guardian and facilitator of the soul of newborn babies into the physical incarnation on Earth. He is present at any birth and also presides over all birthdays.

Ezekiel inspires innovators in all fields to manifest their ideas into reality. He is the well spring of new creativity, new ideas and new invention. He takes an active part in all human endeavors that attempt to improve the human condition on Earth.

Ezekiel is always encouraging you to rise above and beyond your dreams. He holds a chalice of golden light that illuminates the darkest horizon. Ezekiel is a messenger of hope when things are at their most dire. Like the first light of a new dawn, Archangel Ezekiel emanates the promise of rebirth.

"Be born again into the light. I am he that makes all things new."

Key word: *Manifestation.*

Red Ray:

Birth

New Innovations

Rise of the Kundalini

Gold Ray:

Encouragement

Hope

Love

Purple Ray:

Answered Prayers

Divine gifts

Spiritual messengers

Gems:

Diamond

Garnet

Purple Jasper

Ruby

Topaz

ARCHANGEL ARIEL

Archangel Ariel is the guardian of the Second Chakra. She also has a special affinity with the Fourth and Fifth Chakras. She emanates with orange light. She will also come in on the rays of green and blue light.

Archangel Ariel comes through with the element of water.

She rules the Second Chakra with planetary influences of the Moon and Venus.

Archangel Ariel wears an orange cape pinned with a diamond star and crescent brooch. Her sword is made of moonlight.

Archangel Ariel mediates the cardinal flow of the energies of procreation and sexual union. She comes in with Divine Mother energy. She is present at all conceptions.

Ask Archangel Ariel for the help in the matter of fertility and childbirth. Archangel Ariel is a great guardian, friend of and aid to midwives, pregnant women, birthing women and mothers. She protects the womb with a spiritual shield of maternal grace.

Archangel Ariel resonates with the emotions of joy and happiness. She is the facilitator of the union of souls.

She opens the door to true love and delight.

Archangel Ariel infuses our souls with the vibration of compassion and love which elevates passionate desire into higher spiritual impulse.

Pray for Ariel's presence in your life when you are in need of comfort and succor. She will ease your sorrows and enfold you in peace. Ariel asks of us that we engage in joyful celebration of Earthly Existence.

"I play on the heart like a harp that resonates with the Celestial Harmonies of the Cosmos."

Key Words: *Joyful Celebration*

Orange Ray:

Conception

Fertility

Happiness

Green Ray:

Comfort

Healing of the Heart

Nurturing

Romantic Love

Blue Ray:

Expressions of the Heart

Marriage Vows

Spiritual Love

Gems:

Amber

Carnelian

Citrine

Coral

Diamond

Malachite

Turquoise

ARCHANGEL GABRIEL

Archangel Gabriel is the guardian of the Third Chakra. He also has a special affinity with the Fourth and the Seventh Chakras. He emanates on a ray of Golden Light.

Archangel Gabriel would also come through on rays of green and rays of amethyst.

Archangel Gabriel's sword is made of Golden Light. He wears a gold cape pinned with a gold sun. He comes through with the element of fire.

"I am the ray of the midday sun. I illuminate your intentions."

Archangel Gabriel is the harbinger of Divine Will. He is the portal which Divine Will unites with Individual Will. Archangel Gabriel protects the link between our identity on the Earthly plane and the identity of our Higher Self.

He oversees the development of the personality and its orientation to others. He helps direct a person to what uniquely defines them.

Archangel Gabriel has infinite patience for the trial and error process of our individuation as we evolve lifetime after lifetime towards our Higher Selves.

He will always heed our prayers for assistance when we need help finding our way back to our True Self as inevitably occurs if we have given way to the base needs and illusions of our ego or if we have fallen slave to addictions or other aberrant behavior.

Archangel Gabriel imparts strength, fortitude, determination and persistence often beyond what we believe ourselves capable of. Like a lighthouse for sailors, Archangel Gabriel shines a powerful beacon of light to guide our souls back to the shore of its human and spiritual purpose.

"I call all sailors home. Follow my light to navigate the way back to dry land. I am the North Star and the Dawn Sun.

I am the compass that points the direction to your port of origin. If you are ever lost, call on me to guide you. The way will be made known to you in the quiet of your meditation and the resonance of your breath as you still your mind and experience the sacredness of your unique soul."

As with all Archangels, Gabriel is a great healer. His presence is a powerful boon and boost to energy healers.

Key words: *Divine Will*

Gold Ray:

Childhood

Prayer

Sacred Places

Green Ray:

Breath

Meditation

Self Love

Amethyst Ray:

Energy Healing

Enlightenment

Past Life Memories

Gems:

Amethyst

Calcite

Emerald

Golden Tiger's Eye

Purple Tourmaline

Yellow Jasper

ARCHANGEL RAPHAEL

Archangel Raphael is the guardian of the Fourth Chakra. He also has a special affinity with the Fifth and Seventh Chakras. He manifests through the heart on the green ray of love. Raphael would also resonate with and manifest on the color rays of blue and amethyst. He unifies all the Chakras through the portal of the Heart Chakra.

Archangel Raphael's sword is made of Sunlight. His cape is emerald green and he fastens it with a brooch in the shape of a golden harp. His staff is also made of gold with an emerald embedded on top in the shape of a sphere.

Archangel Raphael comes through with the element of water. He is the portal through which Individual love and Divine Love meet and merge.

"I am the message and the messenger that tells the story of your heart to the Universe."

Archangel Raphael's frequency vibrates with the alchemical resonance of spiritual transformation. It dissolves fear and opens the heart to trust that all will be well if one allows a quiet space within to bask in the protection of Divine Grace.

"I am the Chalice. I am the cup of love that runneth over. I am the highest reach and the widest span of all your hearts desires. There is no beginning and no end to my love.

Know me through the abundant nature of Universal Love which is your birthright as a Divine Child of the Highest of the High."

Archangel Raphael allows you to know love in its purest vibration. He will come to you whenever you are in need of his assistance in all matters of the heart. Meditate on expanding the vibration of your love to encompass compassion for all sentient beings as you surrender to the all encompassing love and compassion of the Universe as it enfolds and comforts you.

Know that Archangel Raphael is always with you and you can always know him when you are being true to your heart. If you feel you have lost touch with your emotional truth, pray to Archangel Raphael and he will illuminate the way back by the light of his own love shinning like a golden torch in the night. All you need to do is ask. Archangel Raphael imparts Divine Love, compassion, gentleness, patience, tolerance and innocence.

Key Phrase: *I Am the Open Heart*

Green Ray:

Empathy

Intentions

Mindfulness

Prayer

Blue Ray:

Channeling

Communication

Community

Friendship

Amethyst Ray:

Divine Guidance

Purification

Spirituality

Universal Love

Gems:

Amethyst

Aventurine

Emerald

Jade

Malachite

Pink Quartz

ARCHANGEL MICHAEL

Archangel Michael is the guardian of the Fifth Chakra. He would also resonate with the Sixth and Seventh Chakras. He manifests through the portal of the throat chakra and the ray of communication, the color of turquoise. Archangel Michael also manifests and resonates via the colors rays of indigo and amethyst.

Archangel Michael's sword is made of White Light. He wears a turquoise blue cape and he fastens it with a diamond brooch in the shape of a lemniscate.

Archangel Michael is also the guardian of the Book of Life, past, present and future also known as the Akashic Records. He is the keeper and protector of Knowledge. He encourages and inspires us to be seekers of Eternal Truth.

Archangel Michael also encourages us to be ever vigilant in how we proceed in relation to others in as much as we ever strive to be fully honest with ourselves regarding our intentions and desires. He asks us to be open to the expression of our true personalities and not be afraid to reveal our true natures to the light of the higher mind's eye.

Archangel Michael requires us to know ourselves and to understand our Divine purpose regarding our Earthly incarnations. He shines the light of illumination on our destiny.

He encourages us to invoke his name in prayer when we feel lost in life and are confused about or cannot find our direction or vocation regarding our true purpose. Call on Archangel Michael to help guide your way with this shinning sword of Divine Light.

Archangel Michael removes obstacles from our path which impede our progress in manifesting our hopes and desires in alignment with our Higher Self. Archangel's Michael's sword cuts through the distortions and illusions that shield and shroud our vision from our higher truth in alignment with Divine Truth.

In this way we can recalibrate our spiritual resonance which allows us to pass through spiritual portals we were previously denied access to. The blindfold of illusion and ignorance that covers our mind's eye to what is possible falls away and we are able to perceive new solutions to previously intractable problems.

Through this process, we are able to shed unnecessary doubt, fear and anger that bind us to the lower vibrational frequency of egocentric attachments.

"I am the way through, the light and the way to the light

My sword shines like a beacon in the night to illuminate that which is hidden in the darkness created by disconnection from your Higher Self.

Call upon me when you need help with spiritual confusion, when you feel unsure of truth that comes from within, when you cannot hear or trust your inner voice and you feel you cannot or are afraid to speak your inner truth.

I will help you find the quiet space within where love and self-expression meet.

Pray to me for the courage to give voice to what stirs within you but you dare not speak in the face of disapproval, derision, rejection and or reprimand.

I will always come at your request.

My love, protection and guidance are always there for the asking."

Key Phrase: *Speaking your truth*

Turquoise Ray:

All forms of creative expression

All instruments

Choir and Group Singing

Cinema

Creative Writing

Journaling

Lecturing

Lyrics

Music

Musical Composition

Novels

Podcasting

Poetry

Prose

Radio

Sermons

Short Stories

Singing

Song Writing

Story Telling

Teaching

Indigo Ray:

Angelic Guidance

Automatic Writing

Channeling

Clairvoyance

Divine Telepathy

Kinesiology

Ley lines

Prayer

Psychic abilities

Sacred Geometry

Scrying

Tarot Reading

Amethyst Ray:

Chakra Realignment

Energetic Shifting

Manifestation

Gems:

Diamond

Fluorite

Sapphire

Sodalite

Turquoise

ARCHANGEL
URIEL

Archangel Uriel is the Guardian of the Sixth Chakra but also resonates and manifests through the portals of the Fourth and Seventh Chakras. He comes through on the the color ray of indigo. He will also manifest through and resonate on the rays of rose pink and violet.

Archangel Uriel's sword is made of Starlight. His cape is indigo blue and fastened with a diamond and sapphire brooch in the shape of a lily which represents the celestial song of the Heavens.

Archangel Uriel opens the alchemical door of the Pineal Gland which allows you to access Universal Knowledge. He is the transmitter of that which is known, past, present and future and also presides over the Akashic Records along with Archangel Michael.

Archangel Uriel is the spiritual guardian of the karmiccords which connect each incarnation to its Higher Self. In some situations, he will manifest as a shepherd gently calling the soul home to join the Cosmic Flock.

Uriel helps us send and receive spiritual messages. He raises our vibration to a higher and faster frequency and in this way assists us to 'lighten up' so we are able to become more effective vessels for this type of ethereal communication.

Archangel Uriel is also the ruler and teacher when it comes to guiding and utilizing our intuition. Pray to Archangel Uriel when it is in your heart to increase this skill. He will give you guidance as to how to still your mind and allow your inner knowing to come to the surface of your awareness.

Archangel Uriel also assists us in increasing our ability to communicate with our Spirit Guides. He will often introduce us to our Spirit Guides in dreams. He acts as the bridge through the energetic, astral and etheric dimensions which link the Spirit World to the Material World.

"I am the night sky and the stars and moon within it.

Heed my words heard only in that sacred space between the night and the dawn, between the sea and the shore, between sound and silence.

I am the Ocean's end and the rivers that run into it.

Hear my voice as they merge theirs with mine.

I am the bird on the wing and the space that embraces it.

I am the great connector and all that is connected, the network and the grid.

I bring the songs of the stars that are always singing to your soul's awareness."

Archangel Uriel helps us communicate with all spiritual beings by purifying and quickening our vibration. As we do so, our Third Eye opens to all manner of beings and environments and illusory veils that separate the dimensions begin to disappear. We can then understand without a doubt that all things, seen and unseen have a spiritual presence and share our planet with us in a multiplicity of worlds within our world.

Archangel Uriel also helps us with *spiritual remembering*, especially with who we were in our past lives as well as the reasons for our choices in between lives that determined the way our current incarnation has manifested.

Key phrase: *Seeing through the eyes of the Soul*

Indigo Ray:

Astral Traveling

Channeling

Clairvoyance

Clairaudience

Communicating with Spirit Guides

Lucid Dreaming

Remembering Past lives

Seeing through the dimensions

Shape Shifting

Telepathy

Rose Pink Ray:

Cleansing

Compassion

Emotional Healing

Eternal Love

Love of nature

Spiritual Healing

Universal Love

Violet Ray:

Co-creating flower essences and other vibrational essences with Nature and Angel Spirits

Communicating with Angels

Meditation

Prayer

Working with crystals

Gems:

Blue Sapphire

Celestine

Chalcedony

Crystal

Quartz

Selenite

ARCHANGEL CHAMUEL

Archangel Chamuel is the Guardian of the Seventh Chakra and also manifests and resonates through the portals of the Fifth and Sixth Chakras. He manifests through the portal of the Crown Chakra at the top of the head and the ray of enlightenment, the color of violet. Chamuel would also resonate with the color rays of turquoise and indigo.

Archangel Chamuel's sword is made of the color spectrum of the Rainbow. His cape is the color of violet and it is fastened with a brooch of amethyst fashioned in the shape of a cobra which represents the rising of the Kundalini to the Crown Chakra and the opening of the Crown Chakra.

Archangel Chamuel opens the gateway to the all knowing part of the Self which is one with all creation. He makes accessible the part of the Self which is external, without end, without attachment to this 'mortal coil' beyond death and rebirth.

Archangel Chamuel helps us open up and align with the harmonic frequencies of the Universe, the highest of vibrations. He teaches us the ability to channel spiritual energies necessary for the transformation of human consciousness. Ask Archangel Chamuel to help you connect with your physical, emotional, mental, astral and etheric bodies so you can truly self actualize into the sentient enlightened being you are meant to be as we experience our incarnations on this planet known as Earth.

You can also ask Archangel Chamuel to help teach you to identify and balance your chakras so your Kundalini Energies can rise in the appropriate manner.

Archangel Chamuel can help you learn how to make connections between your emotions and your actions so that you can become less reactive and more measured in your interactions with yourself and others.

Reach out to Archangel Chamuel to learn how to make connections between past and present life Karma. Archangel Chamuel can often help you through dreams when you have memories of past life experience filtered through flashes of insight as you go in and out of your dream cycles. He can also assist you in this way during past life regressions and other methods of past life discovery.

Archangel Chamuel can help guide the soul to the "other side" when it takes leave of its physical body and makes its transition to the world of pure spirit. Pray to Archangel Chamuel when the time of departure is near, for a loved one, human or animal for safe passage and he will come to assist the journey through the veils to our soul's home.

"I am the channel that connects you with your Higher Self and all Being.

I am the light that illuminates your darkness and reveals to you the splendor of the Universe you inhabit and removes all of your illusions so that you can perceive it with true Spiritual Vision.

I am the portal through which you receive the gift of enlightenment."

Key Phrase: *Finding Enlightenment*

Violet Ray:

Chakra work

Channeling Spiritual Energy

Communication with spirits who have passed

Raising of the Kundalini

Spiritual Healing and Spiritual Passage

Indigo Ray:

Breath Work

Light Working

Meditation

Prayer

Psychic predictions

Turquoise Ray:

Emotional Expression through Poetry, Lyrics and Prose

Marriage Vows

Spiritual Beliefs

Spiritual Books and Tomes

Gems:

Amethyst

Celestite

Chalcedony

Diamond

CHAPTER FOUR
MORE THOUGHTS ON DIVINE TIMING

Time itself and the passage of time is a very paradoxical human concept. On one hand, it is an absolute measured by events and the sequence of events whether it is recorded by the ticking of a clock or the revolving of the sun around the planet. There are sixty seconds in a minute and we start a new year every 365 days according to the Roman calendar.

However, the sun itself varies in the time it takes to revolve around the earth,(hence the Octavian leap year) as do the other planets and although the count of seconds, minutes and hours do not alter, our perception of their passing certainly does. Everyone experiences and remembers the passing of time differently.

Depending on our perception, it can slow down, speed up or even be perceived to have stopped.

Albert Einstein, the father of modern physics, famously theorized that time is relative to the speed of light and can run faster or slower depending on how high in space you are and how fast you are travelling. How do the Angels perceive time? Very relatively! In Divine Consciousness, the perception of time can be compared to water. It is the lapping of the waves on the shore. It is the furious pace of the rapids and the stillness underneath. It all flows to the same ocean yet its journey varies with the life path of each soul.

Aligning our resonance to Divine Timing helps us let go of our limited expectations and concepts of the timing within which we think things should happen and experience time in a more fluid way. It allows us to accept that time is elastic in its ability to expand and contract, and also ponder the possibility that we can live as fully in a moment as in a whole year. It is all about perception!

Being in alignment with Divine Timing assists us to understand intuitively that all things happen in their own 'time 'and that if we allow ourselves to accept the grace of Divine Synchronicity in which there is always a higher purpose and wisdom to how the sequence of the events of our lives unfold. Divine Timing will always orchestrate the unfolding of its manifestation in alignment with our higher good and the good of all.

When we transmit our prayers to the Angels, so often time is a concern. We may be praying on a matter where time is of the essence: money that we need to pay our rent or medical bills, getting to the hospital on time, getting an assignment done on time, getting a new job, finding a romantic partner and so on. But we need to remember that part of the condition of prayer is surrender. We shoot our arrow of prayer out to the Universe and then we can only hope that it will be answered as we desire. There is no guarantee. This does not mean the Angels are not hearing our prayers but there are times when Divine Timing is not going to line up with the time parameters we perceive as necessary or desirous.

The Angels and Divine Consciousness as well as our Higher Selves are most concerned with our highest good and beyond that the highest good of all. They are seeing things from a larger and more complex perspective and cannot and will not deviate from that perspective. Yet anyone who has experienced the miracles of their prayers can bring will testify of how their prayers were answered in a miraculous time and right in the 'nick of time.'

One personal story this brings to mind is that of a friend of mine who was stung by a yellow jacket while we were visiting a cider mill with her five-year-old twins. She went into anaphylactic shock just after she complained of not feeling well and pulled over to the side of the road of a small subdivision. This was before the time that cell phones were popular and I had to decide very quickly whether to stay with her or take her two little children with me and quickly find someone to help. It might have been the third or fourth door that I knocked on when finally someone opened, took us in and called an ambulance.

During that time, I remember silently praying to my Angels that we would get help fast and that she would be okay. It seemed to take ages for the ambulance to come but in that time a small crowd had gathered around her and out of the blue a passing Emergency Room Nurse had stopped and taken control of the situation. The nurse tended to her until the ambulance appeared. It was such a small suburb and the odds of a medical professional passing through and stopping at that time seemed pretty small. Whether my prayer assisted that situation or not, that nurse was truly an Earth Angel in my mind and my prayer had been answered in the nick of time. It turned out that my friend still had the stinger of the bee in her thigh and getting to the hospital when she did was paramount to her survival.

Perhaps as we pray and time is one of our concerns, which it is more often than not, adding the caveat of for our highest good regarding timing will help us give our prayers over to the Higher Powers. It is more helpful not to expect our prayers to be answered in the time we wish but at the same time know we can always ask and be grateful when they are.

Some may ask: "So why pray at all if we cannot have what we want when we want it and why accept with love and gratitude a prayer that is not fulfilled in the time we wish or in the way it?" First of all, prayer in itself, regardless of whether it is answered in the way and in the time we wish, is vital in allowing angelic energy to exist on the planet. Because of free will, Angels can only intervene on the majority of matters if we ask them to and if we give them permission.

Prayer and especially prayers that are made with an unconditional intent become our bridge to Divine Consciousness and Will allowing the Angels to be able to be active and manifest in our lives. Prayer is truly resonant when it is expressed with an open heart, an open hand and an open mind. Prayer is like the striking of a match to the candle. It allows us to focus and lift our vibration to the vibration of Divine Light and we become a channel for Divine light as we pray. Our life force becomes intertwined with it. So if and when we become impatient and the answers to our prayers seem delayed, ponder on the cosmic overview, the play of our own personal and also collective karma as well as what is known and yet to be revealed as we surrender to Divine Timing and have faith that all is unfolding in accordance with the Highest Good.

CHAPTER FIVE
A BRIDGE OF LIGHT

The Archangels want to remind us that prayers exist in a myriad of forms worldwide and through all of human existence and that they have always been a bridge of light and connection between humans and the Highest of the High. There seems to have always been a need for human beings to raise their voices and hearts to the Divine in gratitude, worship and entreaty in the form of the secret prayer of the heart or the prescribed prayer of a congregation said en masse.

Prayer predates any written language. My spirit guides tell me that humans, Angels and the Divine Creator/Source have always perceived and communicated which each other since sentient beings incarnated on this earth. Prayer was always the vehicle of communication to and with the Divine Energies, through a plethora of acts including dance, drumming, song, ritual, chanting, poetry, meditation, mantras, incantation, or simply through thought. The ringing of bells, the call of the ram's horn, the lighting of incense and burning of essential oils have all been used for millenniums to lift us up to the vibration of prayer. We know this culturally through ancient art and architecture, revered holy sites, anthropological digs, sacred geometry and religious practices.

One of the first known evidence of inscribed prayer is the 2600 BCE Mesopotamian Kesh Temple Prayer exultations to Nippur and other Sumerian gods and goddesses (Mark 2023).The Dead Sea Scrolls (approximately 200 AD) were wholly dedicated to prayer and prescriptions on how to pray and when. According to Penn State Scholar Daniel Falk (Winner 2016):

"*Even in synagogue liturgy, prayer doesn't have the same meaning as it does for this group, where they're carrying on this cosmic battle...I think for them prayer as warfare was very meaningful and very real. They had a sense, which I think was carefully nurtured, of joining with the angels and in the process, they helped establish a form of group action and a way of relating to God that influenced later religious practice throughout the world.*"

The Angels want to hear our prayers and they want to work with us to manifest them if they are for the highest good. In fact, answering our prayers is a very important part of the Angels service to humanity. A very useful prayer that I would recommend is simply ask for the wisdom and guidance to know what is in your best interest to pray for.

Prayers always initiate a conversation with our Angels even if we do not feel them around us. Prayers connect us with our Higher Self and the Divine. They require focus, intention, detachment and at the same time love and sincerity. They ask us to give ourselves over to Divine Will, Divine Light and Divine Love so that they can be heard loud and clear without expectation, entitlement or ego.

Prayers are an invitation to the Angels to be part of our lives. We are giving them permission to do service for humanity which is why they are here with us. They have complete respect for the Spiritual Law of Free Will that has been gifted to humans so be mindful that they do need our permission to intervene in most matters. Keeping that in mind, prayers open up possibilities that can quantum miracles in our lives.

Prayers in their highest manifestation are the bridge of light that connects us with and lifts us up to the highest vibrations of our souls so that we may have a relationship with our Angels. The Angels themselves are the bridges of light that allow our prayers to traverse to the Divine. This is how, we, ourselves, become bridges of light. How wonderful and awe inspiring it is to converse with the Angels!

CHAPTER SIX
SOME WAYS TO AUGMENT PRAYER

"Mindfulness can help you pray intentionally. The meditative practice of acknowledgment and acceptance is intricately related to prayer. In fact, prayer is a type of mindful activity that allows you to focus intently on forming a deeper, more intimate connection with divine."

-   Paritah Shaw (2019)

Augmenting or enhancing prayer really means finding ways to center yourself, clear your mind, become mindful and raise your vibration so that you can focus and direct your prayer to the angels without emotional 'noise' or mental clutter. Included in this chapter are three very powerful ways to augment prayer, even in times of crises, emotional upset or even panic. These methods include counting breaths channeled from the Angels, the Dr. Bach flower essences and practicing detachment.

COUNTING BREATHS THAT AUGMENT PRAYER

My Guides gave me instruction on how to use certain Yogic breaths to enhance meditations that augment prayer. Do them the way you would do any breath during meditation. Sit in a comfortable position. Quiet your mind. Breathe in gently through your nose. Hold for a few seconds and then exhale through your nose. Repeat the breath with the same count and rhythm. You can start with just a few minutes and then extend out for twenty minutes or more.

BREATHS THAT RESONATE WITH THE ARCHANGELS

Clearing Breath: Helps clear the mind and the heart. Helps you connect with your Higher Self. Aligns all the chakras.

Inhale to the count of eight. Exhale to the count of eleven.

Resonates with Archangel Ezekiel

Peaceful Breath: Calms you down when you are anxious. Helps you 'catch your breath'.

Inhale to the count of seven. Exhale to the count of seven

Resonates with Archangel Ariel

Joyful Breath: Fills the heart with joy. Lifts the mood. Imparts buoyancy to the soul. Opens and links the third, fourth and six chakras. This is a good breath to use when giving gratitude and thanking the angels.

Inhale through the solar plexus to the count of nine. Exhale through the nose to the count of eleven.

Resonates with Archangel Gabriel

Healing Breath: Helps harmonize the flow of Chi in the body. Helps you access the higher Cosmic Sacred Energies to assist with healing on the spiritual, psychological, emotional and physical planes. Aligns and links all chakras.

Inhale to the count of ten. Exhale to the count of nine.

Resonates with Archangel Raphael

Sacred Breath: Brings you into a higher consciousness. Opens and links the fourth, fifth, sixth and seventh chakras.

Inhale to the count of eight. Exhale to the count of seven.

Resonates with Archangel Michael

Transcendent Breath: Pineal Gland Toner. Raises your vibration and aligns it with the vibration of Divine Consciousness. Helps to synchronize the breath with the oscillation of the Universal Heartbeat. Aligns all the chakras with the Metaversal Chakras.

Inhale in to the count of ten. Exhale to the count of seven.

Resonates with Archangel Uriel

Opening Breath: Helps open the Crown Chakra. Assists the individual with being a clear and resonant channel for the new spiritual energies that are shifting us into a higher consciousness at this time in our evolutionary ascension into the Aquarian Age. Opens and links the fourth chakra with the seventh chakra.

Inhale to the count of eleven. Exhale to the count of ten.

Resonates with Archangel Chamuel

Heart Breath: Harmonizes all the physiological systems. It helps center us.

Inhale to the count of five. Exhale to the count of five.

Resonates with all the Archangels

Meditation Breath: Enhances all meditation practice. Allows the chatter of the 'monkey' mind to ease and the stillness of the 'Buddha' mind to deepen.

Inhale to the count of nine. Exhale to the count of seven.

Resonates with all the Archangels

Have patience with the process. Choose the counting rhythm that is comfortable and in synchronicity with you. Experiment, observe, relax, enjoy and most of all trust in your own judgment. You will know what works for you!

USING BACH FLOWER ESSENCES TO AUGMENT PRAYER

What are flower essences? Flower essences are energetically charged plant and water based homeopathic type remedies that help shift emotional, psychological and spiritual blockages so that we can more easily experience healthier and more harmonious states of awareness and attunement. They were invented by Dr. Edward Bach, an English Homeopath who believed that many physical illnesses first manifest on the emotional and psychological planes in the form of irrational beliefs and negative emotional states.

According to Dr. Bach (Bach, Wheeler 1998):

"The action of these remedies is to raise our vibrations and open up our channels for the reception of our Spiritual Self, to flood our natures with the particular virtue we need, and wash out from us the fault which is causing harm. They are able, like beautiful music, or any gloriously uplifting thing which gives us inspiration, to raise our very natures, and bring us nearer to our Souls: and by that very act, to bring us peace, and relieve our sufferings.

They cure, not by attacking disease, but by flooding our bodies with the beautiful vibrations of our Higher Nature, in the presence of which disease melts as snow in the sunshine."

Although today there are literally hundreds of flower essence distributors and as many flower remedies as there are indigenous flowers on earth, the original Bach remedies consist of 38 flower essences, all from flowers and tree blossoms except for Rock Water which Bach derived from a Sacred spring in Wales near his family retreat. Each essence hones in on a specific mental or emotional imbalance that cover the range and variations of emotions from anger, fear, depression, grief and guilt.

Each of the seven mentioned Archangels in this book resonate with a specific Bach Flower Essence and also can be very beneficial for prayer overall.

ARCHANGEL EZEKIEL

Rock Water

Archangel Ezekiel resonates with the one essence that Bach made from Sacred Well Water. It assists with the flow of the life force which, when one is blocked off or stuck, can disconnect the individual from their Higher Self and can also impede their ability to connect or feel connected to the Divine. The mantra for this essence according to Ezekiel is *"I am one with the flow of life"*.

ARCHANGEL ARIEL

Cerato

Archangel Ariel resonates with the Cerato flower essence because Cerato assists with inner listening. It encourages our connection with our intuition which is one of the ways the Archangels as well as our other spirit helpers communicate us. So often, when we hear that small quiet inner voice, it is their guidance that is coming through. Cerato also helps us better recognize the resonation of the angelic voice and helps us tell the difference between what is coming from our own thoughts and what is coming to us from the Angels. The mantra of this flower essence is:*"To listen to divine guidance, I go within."*

ARCHANGEL GABRIEL

Centaury

Archangel Gabriel resonates with Centaury flower essence because Centaury helps us strengthen our solar plexus and assists in establishing a healthier and more harmonious relationship with our individual will and how we define, express and defend our boundaries. Every human being has a divine right to be the Sun in their own Solar System. To sit in right relationship on the throne of our own power assists us to be grounded in the expression and resonance of our prayer to the Angels. Self-esteem, self-love and self- worth, though generated in the heart, are all seated and expressed through the third charka which Gabriel guards. The mantra of Centaury Essence is: *"Divine Light shines through me and I am one with Divine Light. I express my will in alignment with Divine Will."*

ARCHANGEL RAPHAEL

Holly

Archangel Raphael resonates with Holly flower essence because Holly helps to raise the vibration of the heart chakra and transmutes the baser emotions of hate, anger, bitterness and jealousy into the higher frequencies of love, compassion, tolerance, understanding and positive regard. For our prayers to truly vibrate in harmony with the vibrations of the Angels and Divine Love they must come from a place of love and good intention generated in our own hearts. The mantra of Holly flower essence is: *"My love is Thy Love. I am one with Divine Love. My intent is to come from the highest intention."*

ARCHANGEL MICHAEL

Larch

Archangel Michael resonates with the Larch flower essence because Larch helps clear blockages of the fifth chakra, the energy portal of self-expression which Archangel Michael guards. If there is an encumbrance of self-expression, then we have trouble manifesting our truth and our creativity. If we feel we are not heard and what we have to say is not worth listening to, we are inhibited in fulfilling our life's purpose to speak our own truth and sing our own unique song. Archangel Michael teaches us that our creative voice is our sword that frees us from the bondage of social conformity and censure when it holds us back from vibrating to our own resonance and perception of our beliefs and dreams in alignment with Divine Will. Larch flower essence assists us in this journey on an emotional and psychological plane strengthening the fifth chakra and helping us heal our insecurities and doubts. Thus, we more strongly believe in ourselves and in the verbalization of our prayers so Archangel Michael can hear them and give us aid in a powerful way.The mantra of Larch flower essence is: *"I can speak my own truth, I can sing my own song and I can shine my own light in harmony with the Universal expression of truth, creativity and justice."*

ARCHANGEL URIEL

Aspen

Archangel Uriel resonates with the Aspen flower essence because Aspen assists with clearing negative psychic attachments from the sixth chakra and the healing of any holes or punctures in our energy field which may make us overly porous and absorbent of toxic or unwanted astral energies on the lower realms of the energetic planes. The sixth chakra is the portal of the Third Eye which communicates to the pineal gland and allows us to 'see' into the higher more esoteric realms of spiritual experience but often fear, superstition, astral congestion and even psychic attack can cause our sixth chakra to spin out of polarity or close down in order to protect the psyche from perceived threats, real or unreal.

Aspen flower essence gently assists in increasing the vibrational tone and frequency of the sixth chakra, easing fear and superstition so we can rise up to the higher realms on the wings of Archangel Uriel and our other Angels feeling safe, secure and protected in our travels. The mantra of Aspen flower essence is: *"I am safe in the arms of the Angels as I float on the clouds of higher consciousness. I am one with Divine Light and Divine Love and all is well."*

ARCHANGEL CHAMUEL

White Chestnut

Archangel Chamuel resonates with the White Chestnut flower essence because White Chestnut balances and quiets the seventh or crown chakra which is the energy portal on the crown of our scalp where our energies and Divine energies intersect and which Archangel Chamuel guards. Often visualized as a lotus on a pond when fully opened, it blooms like a flower in the Divine Sun radiating to its celestial light. It is what we experience when we are fully in our meditation, at one and in harmony with Divine Consciousness, where we can forget ourselves and become one with the One. White Chestnut flower assists in quieting and calming the mundane, busy and often noisy thoughts that can agitate the still quiet state of consciousness necessary for coming into oneness with our Higher Selves and Higher Mind. It is in that state, we can truly experience peace and transcendence of consciousness. This transcendent state is the place where Archangel Chamuel can help our prayers become better aligned with the vibration and intent of whole of Divine Awareness and it is where mental chatter, worry, anxiety, fears and doubt melt away. The mantra of White Chestnut is: *"My mind is a quiet and still pond ready to receive the grace of wisdom, well being and peace from Divine Guidance and Divine Love."*

Other Flower Essences for General or Specific Uses to Augment Prayer

For panic that interferes with concentration on prayer: *Clematis, Rescue Remedy, Star of Bethlehem*

For anxiety and fear that interferes with focus: *Clematis, Five-Flower Formula, Mimulus, Rock Rose*

For depression that creates a barrier from prayer: *Gorse, Mustard, Sweet Chestnut, Wild Rose*

For feelings of bitterness regarding life's circumstances that seem unfair, frustration, 'what's the point?' *Gentian, Gorse, Willow*

For feelings of unworthiness: *Larch, Pine, Wild Rose*

When praying for a sick loved one or pet: *Five- Flower Formula, Gentian, Red Chestnut*

For a chattering mind, compulsive thoughts, thoughts that get in the way: *Aspen, Cherry Plum, White Chestnut*

When feeling impatient, prayers are not being answered fast enough: *Gentian, Impatiens, Willow*

For feeling overburdened, weighed down, overwhelmed: *Elm, Gentian, Hornbeam, Oak Red, Chestnut*

When feeling overwhelmed or stuck in anger: *Agrimony, Cherry Plum, Holly*

When feeling uncertain, not sure what to pray for; what is the right direction?, what is the right choice?: *Cerato, Larch, Scleranthus*

I highly encourage you to look more into the Dr. Bach Flower Essences, their meanings and uses. Besides Dr Bach's seminal work *The Twelve Healers* included in the Bach Flower Remedies

(Bach Wheeler 1998), I have included several flower essence books suggested for further reading in the reference section at the back of the book which are also excellent resources on how to use the Dr. Bach and other flower essences.

The Dr. Bach Flower Essences can be easily found in your local health food stores, online at Amazon or other online vitamin outlets and also Flower Essence Services which sell the Healing Herbs brand of the original Dr. Bach Essences.

PRACTICING DETACHMENT TO AUGMENT PRAYER

> *"Detachment is not about refusing to feel or not caring or turning away from those you love. Detachment is profoundly honest, grounded firmly in the truth of what is."*
>
> - *Sharon Salzburg (2013)*

Learning to practice detachment is a great way to augment prayer. If we allow ourselves to catch our breaths, connect with our centers and to our Higher Selves, we can focus on delivering our prayers to the Angels and Divine Consciousness without bringing doubt, demand, or impatience as a condition that the Angels may or may not be able to fulfill.

As discussed in the chapter on Divine Timing, as much as we desire our prayers to be heard and manifested, there are other factors that may come to bear regarding their realization and their timing. Perhaps it is not the right time for the manifestation of our prayers or what we pray for may not be for the highest good for ourselves and others, no matter how well intended. Perhaps there is a need to learn from, resolve or transcend that matter on which we are praying before the prayer can be answered. It is helpful to reflect on the concept of karma which exists so that we may learn what is necessary in order to spiritually evolve which is one of the primary reasons we are here. As much as we wish we could avoid a challenge or a difficulty, the very thing we wish to move past could be one of the grains of sand in our paths that help sculpt our earthly natures into pearls.

Meditation, counting breaths, flower essences, mantras, even just smelling a flower, looking at sky or taking a walk in nature can be helpful to clear our minds, come into the present and come back to our prayer and our intentions. When we practice detachment, we can free ourselves from the whirling thoughts and emotions that tend to take our focus and concentration away from our true intent. It only takes a few minutes, even seconds, to step away from an impulse or situation and find balance. Just like an archer might use detachment to narrow in on its target and take aim, detachment can also help us let the arrow of prayer go from its bow of personal intent and surrender it to the Divine. If we pray in this mindful manner, we learn to trust that our prayers will be answered in the best possible timing in the best possible way for the highest good of all.

Prayer and the Zodiac Signs

Aries: The Inspiration

Taurus: The Expression

Gemini: The Thought Process

Cancer: The Emotional Tone

Leo: The Performance

Virgo: The Organization

Libra: The Beauty

Scorpio: The Meditation

Sagittarius: The Aspiration

Capricorn: The Altar

Aquarius: The Hope

Pisces: The Union

PRAYER FOR HEALING AS CHANNELED BY THE ANGELS TO THE AUTHOR

I am washed clean in Divine Light

I am washed clean in Divine Love

I am purified in Divine Light

I am purified in Divine Love

I am renewed in Divine Light

I am renewed in Divine Love

I am shielded by Divine Light

I am shielded by Divine Love

I am protected by Divine Light

I am protected by Divine Love

I radiate at the frequency of Divine Light

I radiate at the frequency of Divine Love

I am blessed by Divine Light

I am blessed by Divine Love

I am healed by Divine Light

I am healed by Divine Love

I am one with Divine Light

I am one with Divine Love

My soul rests safe and eternal in the arms of my creator and I am made whole again.

Prayer Journal

Your prayer journal is a space for you to journal your experiences with prayer, save the prayers that are meaningful to you and also compose your own prayers.

Prayer Journal

BIBLIOGRAPHY

Bach, Edward, and J. F. Wheeler. 1998. *The Bach Flower Essences Remedies, First Edition.* New York, NY: McGraw Hill.

Chambers, O.S. 1935. *My Utmost for His Highest.* U.S.A.: Dodd, Mead and Company.

Diocese of St. Peters. n.d.*A Prayer to Saint Michel, Gabriel and Raphael.* https://dosp.org/our-faith/prayers/a -prayer-to-saint-michael-gabriel-and-raphael-archangels/Accessed July 17,2023.

Hopler, W. 2017. "Jewish Guardian Angel Prayer." *Learning Religions. Com.* https://www.learningreligions.com/jewish-guardian-angel-prayers-124055. Accessed August 3, 2023.

Hopler, W. 2019. *Acknowledging Guardian Angels in Islam: How Muslims Incorporate Guardian Angels in Prayer,* http://www.learningreligions.com/muslim-guardian-angel-prayer-124056.

Lamott, Anne. 2005. *Plan B: Further Thoughts on Faith.* New York: Riverhead Publishers.

Maclean, Dorothy. 1980. *To Hear the Angels Sing.* Hudson, New York: Lindesfarne Press.

Mark, Joshua J.. 2023. "Kesh Temple Hymn." *World History Encyclopedia.* https://www.worldhistory.org/article/2193/kesh-temple-hymn/Accessed July 20, 2023.

Montgomery, L. M. 1908. *Anne of Green Gables.* Montgomery, Alabama: L. C. Page and Co.

Salzberg, Sharon. 1995. *Loving Kindness:The Revolutionary Art of Happiness.* Boulder, Colorado: Shambhala Publications.

Shah, Parita. 2019 On Mindfulness. *Chopra.Com.* https://www.chopra.com/bio/2019/mar/08/parita-shah.Accessed August 7, 2023

Thompson, P. n. d. "Ancient Prayers and Invocations." *https://www.academia.edu/35936666/Ancient_Egyptian_prayers_and_invocations.* Accessed June 3, 2023

Winner, C.. 2016. "The Genesis of Prayer: The Dead Sea Scroll and the Origins of Modern Worship." *Psy.Edu.* http://www.psy.edu/news/research/story/genesis-prayer/Accessed May 1, 2023.

Zeitgeist Musings. 2012. "Beautiful Ancient Prayers."Zeitgeist Musings.Wordpress.Com.*https://zeitgeistmusings.wordpress.com/2012/05/21/a-few-truly-beautiful-prayers/*Accessed July 16, 2023.

WEBSITES

http://www.uphs.upenn.edu/pastoral/pubs/blue.html

Facebook post by Sharon Salzberg from Dec 04, 2013 ⎘

https:// www.coramdeo-in.com/a-primer-on-ancient-prayer/of the Lord of creation. Accessed August 15, 2023.

SUGGESTED READINGS

Allen, Sue. 2007. *Spirit Release: A Practical Handbook.* Alresford, UK: John Hunt Publishing, Ltd.

Bradford, Michael. 1993. *The Healing Energy of your Hands.* Berkley, Ca.: Crossing Press.

Bach, Edward, and J. F. Wheeler. 1998.*The Bach Flower Essence Remedies, First Edition.* New York, NY: McGraw Hill.

Bear, Jessica, and Tricia Lewis. 1998. T*reating Animal Illnesses and Emotional States with Flower Essence Remedies.* Atlanta: Richman Rose Publishing.

Cooper, Diana. 1996. *A Little Light on Angels*. Forres, Scotland: Findhorn Press.

Cooper, Diana. 1997. A *Little Light on Ascension.* Forres, Scotland: Findhorn Press.

Davis, Winnifred. 2022. *Another World Through the Eyes of the Soul: History, Journey and Restoration of the Soul.* Mississauga: Naazima Inc.

Gawain, Shakti. 1978. *Creative Visualization.* Mill Valley, California: Bantam New Age Books.

Gurudas.1989.*Flower Essences and Vibrational Healing.*LA: Cassandra Press.

Kaminsky, Patricia and Richard Katz. n. d..*Flower Essence Repertory.* Nevada City, California: The Flower Essence Society.

Maclean, Dorothy. 1980. *To Hear the Angels Sing.* Hudson, NY: Lindesfarne Press.

Salzberg, Sharon. 1995. *Loving Kindness: The Revolutionary Art of Happiness.* Boulder, Colorado: Shambhala Publications.

Scheffer, Mechthild. 1988. *Bach Flower Therapy: Theory and Practice.* Rochester, Vermont: Healing Arts Press.

Scheffer, Mechthild.1999. *The Encyclopedia of Bach Flower Therapy.* Rochester, Vermont: Healing Arts Press.

Sherwood, Keith. 2005. *Chakra Healing and Karmic Awareness.* St. Paul, MNN: Llewellyn Publications.

ThichNhat-Hahn. 2006. *Walking Meditation: Easy Steps to Mindfulness.* Louisville, Co.: Sounds True Publications.

Weeks, Nora, Victor Bullen, and Saffron Walder. (1964) 1990. *The Bach Flower Remedies Illustrations and Preparations.* Essex, UK: The C. W. Daniels Company Limited.

ACKNOWLEDGEMENTS

The manifestation of *A Bridge of Light: How to Pray to Angels* into a book has been quite a journey. I want to acknowledge my mother, Harriet Sklar, whose life and passing gave me the life force and determination to carry on her flame. I also want to thank Winnifred Davis, my great friend, author, mentor, editor, motivator and fellow visionary whose kind guidance, understanding, patience and sharp eye for detail gave me inspiration, form and grounding to help turn my dream into a reality. Finally, I give great thanks and gratitude to the Angels as always who graciously allowed me to be a bridge of light for them.

ABOUT THE AUTHOR

Melissa R. Sklar is a Professional Psychic Reader and Medium, Channeler, Flower Essence Practitioner and Spiritual Counselor with a background in Mental Health and over twenty five years cumulative experience. She also has a presence on YouTube as Melissa Free Range Psychic and maintains the Sacred Fire Psychic Readings Facebook page. She currently resides in Southeastern Michigan where she continues to practice her craft.

Made in the USA
Columbia, SC
10 April 2024